P9-CDH-238

Benjamin Franklin

GIANTS OF SCIENCE

Leonardo da Vinci

Isaac Newton

Sigmund Freud

Marie Curie

Albert Einstein

Charles Darwin

Benjamin Franklin

Benjamin Franklin

By Kathleen Krull

Illustrated by Boris Kulikov

Viking

An Imprint of Penguin Group (USA) Inc.

VIKING
An imprint of Penguin Young Readers Group
Published by the Penguin Group
Penguin Group (USA) Inc.
375 Hudson Street
New York, New York 10014, U.S.A.

USA / Canada / UK / Ireland / Australia / New Zealand /
India / South Africa / China
Penguin Books Ltd, Registered Offices: 80 Strand, London WC2R 0RL, England

For more information about the Penguin Group visit www.penguin.com

First published in the United States of America by Viking,
an imprint of Penguin Young Readers Group, 2013

LIBRARY OF CONGRESS CATALOGING-IN-PUBLICATION DATA
Krull, Kathleen, author.
Benjamin Franklin / by Kathleen Krull ; illustrated by Boris Kulikov.
pages cm. — (Giants of science)
Audience: 10 plus.
Audience: Grades 4 to 6.
Summary: "Kathleen Krull sheds new light on the Benjamin Franklin—who considered science his true
calling in life, not nation building—in this perceptive, fair-minded portrait."— Provided by publisher.
Includes bibliographical references and index.
ISBN 978-0-670-01287-9 (hardcover)
1. Franklin, Benjamin, 1706–1790—Juvenile literature. 2. Scientists—United States—Biography—
Juvenile literature. 3. Inventors—United States—Biography—Juvenile literature. I. Kulikov, Boris,
date– illustrator. II. Title. III. Series: Krull, Kathleen. Giants of science.
Q143.F8K78 2013   509.2—dc23   2013018404

Printed in LTC Kennerley   Book design by Jim Hoover

1   3   5   7   9   10   8   6   4   2

To Susan Cohen and Brianne Johnson
—K.K.

Benjamin Franklin

CONTENTS

INTRODUCTION   10

CHAPTER ONE
The Swimmer   17

CHAPTER TWO
The Runaway   27

CHAPTER THREE
Extraordinary Ambition   32

CHAPTER FOUR
How to Keep Warm   41

CHAPTER FIVE
Electric Picnics?   48

CHAPTER SIX
Lightning Strikes   59

CHAPTER SEVEN
And More   70

CHAPTER EIGHT
Wrong Turns, Right Turns,
and Funny Turns   79

CHAPTER NINE
In His Spare Time   85

CHAPTER TEN
Franklinmania   90

CHAPTER ELEVEN
Under the Mulberry Tree   99

CHAPTER TWELVE
Lasting Impact   105

SOURCES   112

INDEX   115

INTRODUCTION

If I have seen further [than other people],
it is by standing upon the shoulders of giants.
—Isaac Newton, 1675

*E*VERY KID IN SCHOOL knows Benjamin Franklin as one of America's most important Founding Fathers. The fun one— buff and muscular in his youth, chubby and balding as he aged. He wrote essays about farting, prided himself on his flirting skills with women, had a quip for any situation, and almost always kept his cool.

But not everyone knows that Ben Franklin is considered America's first scientist. For his discoveries and theories about electricity, he looms large in the history of physics. It was science—and his passion for it—that kept him alive and active until age eighty-four and made him sorry to leave this earth. He understood that life-changing discoveries would be made that he unfortunately wouldn't be around to see. "The rapid progress *true* science now makes occasions my regretting sometimes I was born so soon," he said.

"Scientist" wasn't even a word in the early 1700s when Franklin was born. A person pursuing questions about the physical world was called a philosopher of nature or natural philosopher. And there was almost no way to be one full-time. A person needed a day job—which for Franklin was printer and publisher—or to be independently wealthy, which he eventually became.

When Ben was born in 1709, there was no United States. The thirteen colonies in America belonged to England. (Ben was one of the first to suggest they unite and separate from the British king.) There were no public libraries, medical schools, or hospitals; even indoor plumbing was rare.

The state of medical care was appalling. Anyone could set himself up as a doctor. During Franklin's teens, only one of the ten doctors in Boston had any university training. Childbirth was so perilous that women risked their lives every time they went into labor. What with diseases like the much-dreaded smallpox (known as the "speckled monster" for the ugly sores it inflicted), the specter of starvation, and harsh winters, most people did not live past forty.

Deadly fires, often sparked by mysterious lightning or open fireplaces, could burn up whole villages. Natural disasters were viewed as punishment from God. Misfortune might be blamed on witches doing the devil's work. (In Salem, Massachusetts, only fourteen years before Franklin was born, scores of people, most of them women, were accused of witchcraft; twenty were executed.)

However, scientific thought was coming to a crossroads. It would veer away from superstition and toward logical theories that could be tested and proven.

In Europe, the Scientific Revolution was under way, the work of Isaac Newton its cornerstone. Newton was the one to show how our universe functions by the laws of mathematics. The period that started around 1650 was known as the Age of Enlightenment, with intellectuals using reason to advance knowledge of our world.

But in the New World, science lagged behind. What passed for a science lecture in the Colonies might flit between topics like Newton's theory of light, eye

diseases, Dr. William Harvey's theory of blood circulation, health tips, and cute performance pieces with
sparks from static electricity.

Franklin was a rational thinker. He was also a man
with a very practical mind. Yes, theoretical questions
fascinated him, but he always sought the useful benefits of science—how life could be made more comfortable, enjoyable, and safe.

Plus, for Ben, all scientific endeavor was pure joy—
his face always wore its happiest expression when he
was discussing questions about the natural world. At
forty-two, when he could afford to retire, he proudly
announced that he would like to give himself "leisure
to read, study, make experiments." Electricity! Health!
Weather! Comets! Blood circulation! Light! Even perspiration! Like an American Leonardo da Vinci, Franklin
was interested in it all.

Unlike many giants of science, Franklin had a good
sense of humor and could even laugh at himself. Not every idea he had was brilliant; some were dead wrong.
His very first triumph was the useful invention of a
new kind of stove, which led to his work with electricity, which led to the famous lightning experiment and
much more.

Before Franklin, electricity was amusing, great for stunts. It was fascinating, but little understood. Most thought it not especially important, possibly a supernatural force. No one, even the great Newton, understood what "electrical fluid" (as electrical current was called then) really was.

Because of Franklin, people came to understand that electricity was a powerful part of nature, up there with gravity, heat, light, motion. His invention of the lightning rod, inspired by his work with electricity, was proof that through science, natural forces could be controlled and everyday life made safer.

So whose shoulders did he stand on? Whom did he learn from? Good question, as Benjamin Franklin was almost totally self-educated. His father, Josiah, was friends with Cotton Mather, the well-known Puritan minister. Mather's belief in witchcraft had fueled the Salem panic of 1692, but he was also into science. He wrote a pamphlet on measles, the scourge that had killed his second wife and three children, and he sent some eighty letters on topics like corn hybrids and medical theories to the most important science group in the world, England's Royal Society. He promoted the study of "the incomparable Sir Isaac Newton," owned three thousand books, and encouraged people to get the new smallpox inoculation to prevent the dread disease. Franklin would often declare Mather a "key influence" on his life.

Although Ben fought with his older brother James, James expanded Ben's mind. James's Boston print shop provided a venue where Ben could polish his considerable writing skills. Plus James's collection of books, including ones on math and navigation, advanced Ben's speedy self-education. Ben read everything he could get his hands on—like the work of Robert Boyle, the British scholar who was laying the foundation for chemistry and investigating the nature of air. He pounced on the work of William Harvey, the English doctor whose 1628 book on the circulation of blood had been a breakthrough in science as well as in medical care.

Later he was indebted to Dutch scientist Pieter van Musschenbroek for the Leyden jar. With a Leyden jar Ben could store an electrical charge and study it. He drew upon the knowledge of his friends—the leading thinkers of his day in America and Europe whose lengthy letters served the same functions for Ben as scientific journals do for scientists today. Ever congenial, Franklin saw himself as a cheerleader for others' work, and they returned the favor.

Above all, Franklin revered Isaac Newton. He never did master the notoriously difficult *Principia Mathematica*, but Newton's *Opticks*—basically a manual for how to conduct experiments—was perhaps the book that pushed Franklin the furthest. From it he learned about the vital importance of the scientific method—observing, building a theory, and doing careful experiments to prove that theory.

So why is Benjamin Franklin's picture on the hundred-dollar bill? Because of his scientific work? Or because of his part in founding the United States?

Certainly, a list of Franklin's political accomplishments would fill a bigger book. And yet he viewed his career as statesman as a leave of absence from his true calling—science. He was always itching to get back to science full-time. Although never shirking the call of duty, he was happy to leave public life behind. He referred to himself as a "free man" after "fifty years' service in public affairs."

Ben Franklin never lost his excitement about science and injected it into everything he did for America.

CHAPTER ONE

The Swimmer

*B*EN FRANKLIN WAS born in a small, crowded house in Boston, Massachusetts, then the largest village of the British colonies, thanks to its bustling harbor. His father, Josiah, was helping add to the population: he had seventeen children—seven with his first wife, and following her death a week after giving birth, ten more with his second wife, Abiah.

Ben was Abiah's eighth child, born on January 17, 1706. In the style of the times, she "hardened off" baby Ben by dunking him in cold water three times a day. With infant mortality as high as it was then—

in Boston, one-quarter of all newborns died within a week—people hoped this practice would make babies hardier and more likely to survive infections.

Josiah supported his brood by making soaps and candles, getting animal fat from slaughterhouses and boiling it with such substances as highly corrosive lye. It was smelly, sweaty work. And in the case of the Franklins, tragic as well. In 1703, baby Ebenezer accidentally fell into a vat of soap and drowned.

Franklin had only two years of schooling, but he honestly couldn't remember a time when he didn't know how to read. His favorite book was *The Pilgrim's Progress* by John Bunyan, with one of its themes being that progress came from gathering knowledge. Abiah called her young son the "mad philosopher," and worried that Ben read too much. How would he earn a living? But for the rest of his life, Franklin saw books as *the* source of wisdom. Knowledge would help him make his way in the world.

He loved to swim in an age when most people, even sailors, didn't know how to. Immersion in water (except for the baby-dunking) was believed to be unhealthy, but as a child Franklin used a book called *The Art of Swimming*, by a French scientist, to teach himself. He realized that swimming was based on a simple scientific principle: If you remember that bodies are lighter than water, you can just relax and float. Ben mastered various strokes and even learned odd stunts like clipping his toenails underwater. Besides the fact that it was fun and developed his strength, swimming was an excellent way to stay clean.

Franklin's very first invention helped him get around in the water faster—flippers for his feet and paddles for his hands. How practical. How useful. One day he thought up a neat trick: to cross a pond quickly, while floating on top of the water, he held on to a kite string and let the kite propel him along. "The greatest pleasure imaginable," he recalled later.

Franklin's parents were both serious people—Puritans, part of the migration to Massachusetts of people who had fled England for religious freedom. (Puritanism was a Protestant movement whose followers wanted to "purify" the Church of England from traces of the Roman Catholic religion.)

Franklin claimed to have learned the most from his father. Josiah could draw, play music, and use tools. Because of Josiah's common sense, neighbors came to him for advice, and he always let his son sit in on these chats. One of Josiah's friends was the famous Puritan preacher Cotton Mather. Mather's wide range of interests included science, and his expertise had won him election to England's Royal Society, the most important club in the world for scientists.

Josiah's fondest wish was for Ben to become a Puritan clergyman like his friend Cotton Mather. Though Ben was apparently left-handed, a trait believed to be a sign of the devil, he was clearly brainy and industrious, showing early leadership skills. And so full of curiosity. As a young boy he scraped together six precious pennies so he could go see the first lion exhibited in America. His proud father sent him off to a good grammar school to prepare him for Harvard

College, which at that time trained the future clergy-men of New England.

Franklin enjoyed school and did well—except in math, which he failed. But after two years Josiah took him out of school. He didn't have the funds to keep his son enrolled and he needed his help in the shop. Also, Josiah may have sensed that Franklin was just not cut out to be a man of the church—too rebellious, perhaps, and not especially pious. Ben was ten when his formal education came to an end.

Franklin despised working in the shop dipping candles, clipping wicks, and stirring animal fat all day. With Boston Harbor so close by, where a thousand ships were registered, it's not surprising that Ben fell in love with the ocean. Far better to have an action-packed life at sea like one of his older brothers, Josiah Jr. But Ben's father was alarmed—a sailor's life was full of such dangers as pirates, shipwrecks, and scurvy and other awful diseases. Indeed, after ten years as a sailor, Josiah Jr. returned to Boston for a family reunion, then set sail and was never seen again—presumably lost at sea.

To steer Ben away from the ocean, his father took him around to the shops of other tradesmen—glassblower, bricklayer, knife maker, silversmith, brass worker, shoemaker, woodworker, leatherworker—to pick a trade.

At age twelve, Franklin chose the trade that seemed most appealing—printing. He became an apprentice to his brother James, who printed whatever jobs came his way—books, news, popular ballads . . . Ben signed legal documents of indenture that bound him to James until he turned twenty-one. James was nine years older and a bit of a tyrant. But he had been to London and knew its sophisticated ways. Franklin always credited his father's influence on him, but James expanded his horizons even more.

The printing business turned out to be a good fit for Ben, requiring both brains and brawn. It was not a job for wimps—lifting the heavy trays of cast-metal letters, setting the type letter by letter, and folding and binding sheets of paper. But it also offered outlets for Ben's creativity. Right away he started writing ballads about pirates and shipwrecks. Even he called them "wretched," but he printed and sold them around town.

When Franklin was fifteen, in 1721, James founded *The New-England Courant*. Only the third newspaper in Boston, it was the first to be independent of British authorities, sometimes getting on the wrong side of the king. Franklin soon began writing for *The Courant*, but under a pseudonym so as not to irritate his already ir- ritable brother. Pretending to be a middle-aged widow named Mrs. Silence Dogood, Franklin left his witty let- ters about current events for James to find and then publish. For Ben, writing was a joy. The fourteen Mrs. Dogood letters became the talk of Boston and increased sales of the newspaper.

James had a decent collection of books, and Ben be- gan a rabid program of self-education. He saved his food allowance to buy other books. In order to have more time to read, he stopped going to church on Sunday. Pu- ritans frowned. But by fifteen he had drifted from the Puritan religion and adopted deism, an Enlightenment belief that God's truths can be found entirely through nature and reason. Deism didn't require church atten- dance. It was faith through science.

Franklin got hold of math books to remedy his ignorance, and he took up *The Spectator*, a smart London magazine that published articles including the latest news about chemistry and physics. He taught himself how to write clear, powerful sentences by rewriting the essays in *The Spectator*—first in prose and then, to challenge himself further, in verse.

Reading about Isaac Newton in the magazine, a man whom *The Spectator* described as being so brilliant he was "like one of another Species!" made Franklin fantasize about someday meeting this genius of geniuses. Although Newton lived until 1727, the young Ben never got to meet his hero.

Meanwhile, the prevention of smallpox was an important health issue in the early 1700s, one often discussed in the pages of *The Courant*. The Colonies were trying to increase their population. Yet frequent epidemics of the disease wiped out large chunks of the populace—almost one out of ten Bostonians in 1721. "Cures" included smearing tar on the face to ward off evil vapors, eating plants that looked like the moon, bleeding, vomiting, and swallowing medicines made with mercury or soap.

Cotton Mather, however, sought a scientific approach to stopping smallpox. He had learned about smallpox inoculation from one of his African slaves, a man named Onesimus. The theory was that inserting a tiny amount of infected material from someone with smallpox under a person's skin would usually cause only a mild case of the disease. And after that, the person would be immune to smallpox.

The concept wasn't popular. Give yourself the disease to prevent the disease? Ridiculous! The idea seemed so dangerous that people threatened to lynch its advocates and actually threw explosive devices into their homes. There was real concern that a program of inoculation would cause riots in the streets of colonial towns.

The Courant came out against inoculation, and so did Boston's only university-trained doctor. Ben was neutral at first. But on his own, he started collecting data about the practice and its growing success rate. He, for one, became convinced.

The question of inoculation wasn't Ben's only quarrel with James. Ben couldn't stand not being his own boss, and the brothers' relationship worsened when James finally learned the true identity of Mrs. Dogood. Ben tried to find work elsewhere, but James poisoned all the printers in Boston against him.

Ben was done with James. So at seventeen, he up and left Boston.

He'd escaped the tyranny of James, who, Ben claimed, used to beat him, but it was hard to imagine a tougher predicament than the one he now faced: how was he to support himself?

He had to start over somewhere fresh, like New York City, three hundred miles away. Even strong and muscular as he'd become, he obviously couldn't swim there. But he could sell some of his precious books. And with that money he could board a ship and escape!

CHAPTER TWO

The Runaway

*T*OO BAD FOR Franklin, New York had
exactly one printer, and he had no need of an
assistant.

So the runaway moved on to Philadelphia, Pennsylvania, which was on its way to outranking Boston
as the most important American port city. Fewer people lived there, so Ben thought finding work might
prove easier. Philadelphia was compelling—an intellec-
tual center, more tolerant than Boston, and cleaner, too,
with leafy parks and wide avenues, though those avenues were still unpaved.

Ben's voyage from New York City to Philadelphia

had been harrowing. The ship he was on foundered, his luggage lost. After taking a ferry to the mainland, he walked the last fifty miles into the city. By this point he was broke, tired, and starving; he cut a pathetic, semi-comical figure—almost six feet tall, with spare socks and underwear stuffed into his coat pockets.

Franklin was determined to reinvent himself the only way he knew how: through serious hard work. He soon found jobs in printing shops around town. Philadelphians took notice of this bright young man who was already in the shop when his bosses got up, and was still working at eleven at night when something needed to get done.

As soon as he had some money in his pockets, Ben couldn't resist visiting his family back in Boston to show off his new clothes and silver watch. James was still furious with him, but in time the brothers reconciled. (Years later, James would even send his young son to work for Ben as a printer's apprentice.)

In Philadelphia, somehow Franklin came to the attention of the Pennsylvania governor and landed an incredible opportunity. The governor sent Ben to London. London! Home of Isaac Newton. Home of the Royal Society. The largest city in Western Europe.

His mission was to buy and bring back equipment to establish another newspaper in Philadelphia.

After an arduous voyage that took three months, it turned out that the governor couldn't actually *pay* for the printing equipment. Ben's mission fizzled, but there he was on the other side of the Atlantic and, ever resourceful, he landed on his feet, working as a typesetter in a printer's shop.

His eighteen months in London were transformational. People liked him and looked after him. After working all day he still found time to attend plays and take part in coffeehouse discussions. He borrowed books. He met men from the Royal Society and read their scientific journals. Though he was far from illustrious and had no chance of joining the society, he still tried to get his foot in the door by selling a specimen of American asbestos—an interesting fireproof substance—for a nice sum to the secretary of the society. All the while he hoped for a glimpse of the mighty Newton, the sitting president of the society. Unfortunately, he never did lay eyes on him.

Showing off his buff body to Londoners, Franklin performed swimming stunts, such as paddling three and a half miles alongside a boat in the Thames River.

Should he turn himself into a theatrical act, he wondered, or open a swimming school?

But those options felt like they would be a waste of his life, and so he finally returned to Philadelphia, still penniless. It was no London; however, it was growing fast and still needed printers. Above all, Franklin wanted to be useful.

In fact, on the three-month voyage home, Franklin wrote "A Plan for Future Conduct." He compiled rules for behavior for himself so that he "may live in all respects like a rational creature." Later he would list thirteen virtues he aspired to—such as moderation, humility, and tranquility—having serious issues with only one: order.

He continued cultivating his mind. His body, too—in calm seas he would stun the sailors by swimming laps around the ship, keeping an eye out for sharks.

And he started his first scientific journal. He recorded observations of the winds, water, a lunar eclipse, rainbows . . . He noted the habits of dolphins, sharks, and every sea creature he observed. He was delighted to find tiny crabs—"each less than the nail of my little finger"—attached to seaweed, and he collected seaweed samples in a glass container for further observation. Determined to "preserve a curiosity" about nature, he aspired to learn as much as he could. Perhaps even to discover something new to add to America's— or the world's—knowledge.

CHAPTER THREE

Extraordinary Ambition

*B*ACK IN PHILADELPHIA in 1726, weakened by the transatlantic voyage, Franklin promptly fell ill with pleurisy, a serious lung infection. He was sick so rarely, and this first brush with mortality scared him. When he recovered, Ben threw himself into work and self-improvement, racking up a rapid series of accomplishments over the next several years.

At twenty-one, he was working in print shops again but was missing the lively company he'd kept in London. He began contacting the smartest men he knew. Inspired by groups that Cotton Mather had founded,

used health and death as topics to grab readers' attention—
the inoculation debate again (he was in favor it), the
causes of the common cold, and every tiny detail about
damage done by lightning storms.

He was becoming a respected man about town,
and it was time to marry. Plus he had the responsi-
bility of a baby—an illegitimate son named William,
whose mother remains unknown to this day. Ben
needed a wife, especially one with a dowry—money
that would help pay off what he still owed on his print
shop. Courting one woman, he tried to persuade her
family to mortgage their house and give the money to
the young couple. That didn't fly. Handsome and industrious as Franklin was, he was not the sort of well-born
catch to attract a young lady of means.

So he went back to the first girl he'd met in Philadelphia. On the day he'd arrived, as he was devouring
his bread, fifteen-year-old Deborah Read had laughed at
him from a doorway, finding him "awkward" and "ridiculous." They had become close, but while he was in
London, she married someone else. That husband had
vanished. To avoid the serious charge of bigamy in case
the husband ever returned, Deborah and Franklin established a common-law marriage in 1730—an informal
union, legal but without a ceremony. Deborah raised

Franklin created the Junto (related to the Spanish word for "joined"). It was a group of "like-minded [men], aspiring artisans and tradesmen who hoped to improve themselves while they improved their community."

The members—twelve to start, of whom Franklin was the youngest—had to swear to their love of truth for truth's sake. Only one man had been to college, at Oxford in England. The others worked in the trades or were just big readers who liked beer. They discussed books and current events in conversations that were wide and free-ranging. They might spend hours trying to define the meaning of wisdom or explain why a glass of beer produced condensation.

At first the group was secret, to keep its membership small, and they met in taverns on Friday nights. (Ben, not a big drinker in an age when everyone else was, preached moderation to the other members.) Later they got their own clubhouse; Franklin was to remain head of the Philadelphia Junto for thirty years.

By 1728, Franklin had set up a print shop of his own. The following year he became the publisher of his own newspaper, *The Pennsylvania Gazette*. Now he had a forum for circulating knowledge as if it were fresh air, and that included discoveries in the sciences. He

William as her own son, and two years into their marriage was also taking care of their first child together, Francis, or Franky.

Deborah lived her whole life within a few blocks of the house on Market Street where she grew up. She could just barely read and write. Franklin didn't mind—he loved women, but he didn't believe in higher education for them, nor did he think that they should "meddle" in politics. He saw Deborah as "a good and faithful helpmate." She sewed his clothes, as well as the bindings on the books he printed, and did the bookkeeping and all the housework until they could afford servants and slaves. Yes, slaves. For many years, Franklin was a man of his times in accepting slavery, though, unlike some other Founding Fathers, he grew to abhor it later in life.

Meanwhile, the Junto members were outgrowing the shelf of books they owned. They needed more. However, books were expensive. So twenty-seven-year-old Franklin came up with one of his best ideas—the first lending library in America. Men had to pay a fee, but anyone could join (though women weren't admitted until 1769). Its lofty motto was "To Pour Forth Benefits for the Common Good Is Divine," and Franklin hired the first American librarian to manage it. Soon

the library boasted more than three hundred books—
all nonfiction, many on science—as well as equipment
like an air pump made famous by Robert Boyle for
learning more about how air functioned. Throughout
his life, Franklin remained immensely proud of what libraries contributed to America. He said they made "the
common tradesmen and farmers as intelligent as most
gentlemen from other countries."

More personally, he read his library's books for
an hour or two every day, taking this "means of improvement by constant study" to make up for his
haphazard schooling. He started collecting encyclope-
dias, sometimes printing excerpts from them, and be-
friended Noah Webster, who encouraged his zeal for
words (so much so that Webster dedicated his *Dissertations on the English Language* to Franklin in 1789). To
keep himself awake during meetings he found boring,
he did mathematical puzzles to polish his math skills.

At his printing company, he published the first
American medical book, *Every Man His Own Doctor:
Or, The Poor Planter's Physician* by John Tennant, a
bestseller in an era when people had to tend to health
problems on their own.

He also began to publish *Poor Richard's Almanack,*

his compendium of useful information, soon the most famous book in the Colonies. It had the sayings that we remember Franklin for, like "No gains without pains," "Haste makes waste," and "Early to bed and early to rise makes a man healthy, wealthy, and wise." In addition, it was a primer for amateur astronomers, with day-by-day descriptions of events in the skies. In it Ben explained what he knew about Newton and Boyle, the latest findings of English astronomer Edmond Halley, and the new sights to be seen with a microscope or telescope. Readers loved it, and he sold enough copies to make him rich.

A superb networker, Franklin cultivated friendships with the best minds in science. One of his closest friends was John Bartram, the Colonies' premier botanist, who had sent more than a hundred new plant species to England. He was also friends with James Logan, a wealthy scholar from Great Britain who brought rare science books (even Newton's thorny *Principia*) to the Colonies. Men like Logan showed their own manuscripts to Franklin for fact-checking before publishing them.

Later, in 1743, Franklin extended his reach beyond Philadelphia and founded the American Philosophical Society to promote "Useful Knowledge among the British Plantations in America." "Useful" was Franklin's watchword, after all. The Society was modeled on England's Royal Society, a group that not only read about new discoveries but had members who were important scientists themselves. It was Franklin's way of extending his Junto concept into other colonies.

Ben Franklin had succeeded in reinventing himself as something truly cool: the leading source of scientific information in America, his very own information superhighway.

At the same time, he was dipping his toes into politics. He'd become the official printer for Pennsylvania, and then for other colonies, which won him more respect and further contacts. In 1736 he served as clerk of the Pennsylvania Assembly, the body that created and passed laws for the colony. Then he was elevated to postmaster for Philadelphia.

At thirty, perhaps exhausted, he fell ill again and almost died.

He recovered, but the following year, his beloved four-year-old son Franky died of smallpox. As much as Franklin supported inoculation, he had delayed inoculating his own child because the boy was recovering from another illness. Franky's death broke Ben's heart, and fifty years later he still cried at the mention of his son's name.

His own illness and his son's death were sharp reminders that time was not limitless; Ben wanted to make his mark, to *do* something with the knowledge he was gaining.

In a letter to his mother he wrote, "I would rather have it said 'He lived usefully' than 'He died rich.'"

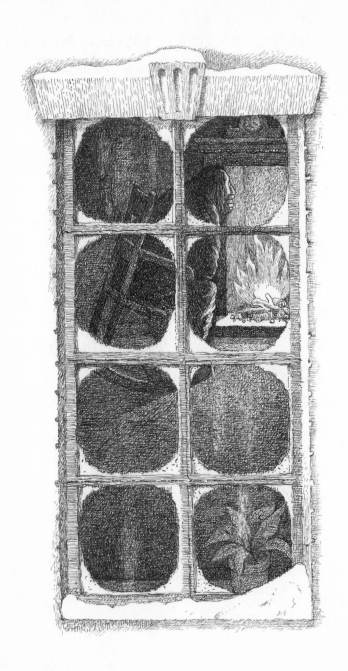

CHAPTER FOUR

How to Keep Warm

EN FRANKLIN WAS not a scientist in the sense of a person coming up with a hypothesis and trying to prove it. Rather, he started with a practical problem and tried to find a solution, and in the process he observed scientific principles at work. And the problem most on Franklin's mind was health. Everyone, not just the Franklin family, suffered from the brutal winters in the Colonies.

The way homes were heated at the time was terribly inefficient. Huddling near traditional open fireplaces meant burning your feet while your rear end remained numb with cold and drafts blew elsewhere around the room. In addition, everyone was breathing smoky, sooty air, which produced coughs, itchy eyes, colds, and diseases.

What would help? Ben started tinkering with home-heating designs around 1740. Others were working on this same problem, but not with the same scientific understanding that Ben possessed. Franklin was keenly interested in how the human body regulated heat. He carried out experiments with a machine he built, verifying for himself William Harvey's finding that the circulation of blood distributed heat within the body. A room was like a body, needing its temperature to be properly regulated.

Without a lab of his own, using his own house instead, Franklin investigated the flow of air, seeing if there was a way to control it. He held a lit candle up to a keyhole to observe the candle flame bending toward the keyhole, showing that the warmth was escaping. He did experiments heating empty bottles, then inverting them in water, observing that as the temperature of the air in the bottle decreased, the air contracted and created space so that water was drawn into the bottle. This demonstrated that warm air took up more space than cold air.

When wood was burned in an ordinary open fire-place, the heat radiated out in a straight line. Since heated air rises, most of the heat went directly up and out the chimney and was quickly lost. Meanwhile, if there were any chinks in the walls or windows, the fire actually pulled *cold* air into the room, because as hot air went out the chimney, cold air rushed in to replace it. According to Franklin, this makes "a continual whistling or howling; and it is very uncomfortable as well as dangerous," causing "colds in the head, rheums, and defluctions which fall into [the] jaws and gums."

Franklin's idea was a new kind of woodburning stove. He would move the fire from an open hearth into a metal box that was inside the fireplace and connected to the chimney. Behind the metal box, he added a "winding passage" of small metal chambers that made hot air travel a longer path and kept it from escaping so quickly. Metal is a good conductor of heat, so the heat in the metal box was captured and radiated into the room, while the smoke was directed into the chimney.

Now instead of crowding near the fireplace, people could move around a room. They could see the fire, which was comforting psychologically—something other enclosed stoves such as the Dutch oven did not afford.

Franklin's stove represented an improvement in comfort, and it was also energy efficient. Franklin worried that the clearing of so many forests in the New World might result in such a terrible shortage of wood that coal for heating would have to be imported from Europe—much too expensive. Franklin's iron stove used one-quarter the amount of wood that a typical fireplace used, he claimed, even though it gave off more heat.

The Franklin stove was a perfect example of how science could improve everyday life. It was useful. It was practical. It was wonderful!

And he was able to invent it because of what he knew about air circulation from the most current scientific research. He was asking scientific questions. Why did air move when heated? What causes motion in air? What is air? Franklin was doing physics in the manner of his idol Newton, helping to show that air— and indeed all matter—was made up of invisible particles, a basic force of nature. He used Newton's language in referring to "rays of heat" and "rays of light" that radiated outward from the fire. He also leaned on Newton for his knowledge of particles. His new

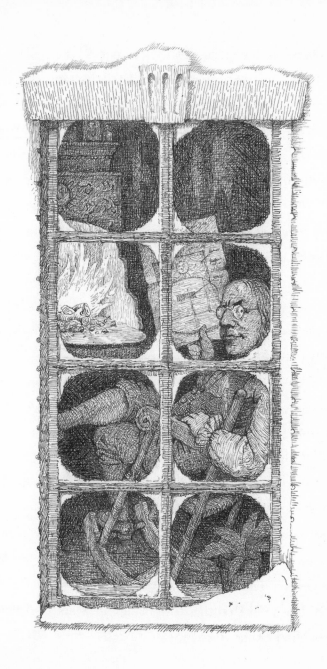

stove was an experiment in how particles circulate.

In 1744, an ironworker and fellow Junto pal assembled Franklin's first "Pennsylvania fireplace." And his first scientific publication was the manual for assembling and using his stove, a 1744 pamphlet called *Account of the New Invented Pennsylvanian Fire-Places.* It had proper footnotes in Latin, the scholarly language, and in its explanations referred to numerous books on natural philosophy.

Ben was immediately offered the chance to patent his design, but he declined: "As we enjoy great advantages from the inventions of others, we should be glad of an opportunity to serve others by any invention of ours; and this we should do freely and generously." He passed up a fortune, as he did again many times in the future. Franklin never patented any of his inventions.

In his newspaper, he marketed the stove himself for the next twenty years. Others made improvements to it, like adding vents, and he himself kept tinkering with the design until the end of his life. The final version, called a Franklin stove, is still in use—a simpler model of Ben's original invention.

Ben's work on the stove made him want to devote much more time to science.

At age forty-two, independently wealthy and with a new baby daughter (Sally), he quit his job as a printer and publisher. He wanted to give himself "leisure to read" and study, and to make experiments, he declared in 1748, "on such points as may produce something for the common benefit of mankind, uninterrupted by the cares and fatigues of business."

What Franklin was fantasizing about was a very private life as a natural philosopher. Soon, though, the tense political situation in the Colonies got in the way and turned him into more of a public figure than ever.

CHAPTER FIVE

Electric Picnics?

ONCERN FOR THE Colonies drew Ben Franklin like a magnet into public life. Politics held appeal as yet another way to be useful. After all, his hero, Isaac Newton, had become a public servant later in life. Newton, however, merely managed money as Warden of the Mint; Franklin eclipsed him in this arena by helping to found a whole new country.

Franklin had taken a keen interest in current events for years. And around the same time that he retired from the printing business, he actively entered the political fray. He made a speech.

Despite his remarkable people skills, public addresses were not his forte. Even he called himself a "bad speaker," with many hesitations and little eloquence. Still, as his accomplishments grew, his opinions held more and more authority. He must have been persuasive on the day in 1748 in Philadelphia that he urged the Colonies to form their own militia, a military force separate from Britain's. After gathering five hundred signatures on the spot he was quickly elected to his first post, as a member of the Philadelphia Common Council, which made laws for the city.

After this he was in such demand as a public spokesman that he had to split his time, staying involved with science as best he could.

He was attracted to one of the greatest mysteries in science at the time—"electrical fluid," as electricity was commonly known. In 1743 he attended lectures in Boston given by the Scottish Archibald Spencer. As part of his performance, Spencer did simple tricks with sparks, or "fire diffused through all space." Intrigued, Franklin promptly brought him to Philadelphia in 1744 and later bought up all Spencer's glass tubes and other equipment.

Was electricity really a type of fire? A liquid? Two

different liquids? A power or "virtue" that could be stimulated? What was it? Not much had been learned for the past 2,400 years, since the ancient Greek philosopher Thales of Miletus had first noted that rubbing amber with fur seemed to make the amber attract other objects. Six hundred years later, the Greek philosopher Pliny the Elder observed the same thing and also mentioned that certain fish produced a shock when touched. It was not until the year 1600 that Queen Elizabeth's doctor, William Gilbert, first used the Latin word *electricus*, which means "coming from amber," to describe the strange force. He performed experiments that increased knowledge about the way electricity behaved and established the fact that electricity could be generated by many substances, not just amber.

The kind of electricity known back then is what we now call static electricity—the harmless phenomenon, experienced most often on dry winter days, of walking across a rug and touching a doorknob, getting a small shock, and seeing a spark. Or pulling off your hat and feeling your hair standing on end. In 1729 Stephen Gray had demonstrated that some substances, such as wire, "conducted" electricity, while other substances, such as glass, did not. Touching a substance that did not conduct electricity was how to prevent yourself from receiving a shock.

Naturally, Franklin would have been familiar with static electricity. But in the eighteenth century, it was interesting mostly as a parlor trick. It was produced on purpose by rubbing two substances against each other. Some tricks were simple, like making bits of paper or metal "jump," or creating optical illusions or tiny explosions. More complex stunts included the "Venus Electrificata," where a woman was secretly charged with electricity and then would shock any man who tried to kiss her. Another performance piece was "The Dangling Boy," from 1730, which featured an electrically charged boy suspended by silk cords from the ceiling while someone drew sparks from his feet or hands. This stunt showed that the human body conducted electricity. Using this knowledge, in 1746, the French priest and physicist Jean-Antoine Nollet sent an electrical shock through a human chain of several hundred monks.

The reason for the electrifying effects perplexed everyone. Newton did not have a lot to say about electricity specifically; he had hypothesized, however, that there was a kind of "elastic fluid" that filled space. He suggested that forces such as gravity moved through this fluid, which he called aether. Franklin wondered if maybe electricity moved through the aether as well.

In Franklin's day, the most popular explanation for electricity was the two-fluid idea. Sometimes electricity seemed to create attraction between two objects, for instance, causing little bits of paper to cling to an electrified object. Sometimes it seemed to make two objects repel each other. So in 1733 the Frenchman Charles François de Cisternay du Fay suggested that there were two different and opposing types of "electrical fluid." One was called "vitreous," because it was created by rubbing glass ("vitreous" means "glassy"), and the other was "resinous" because it was created by rubbing resins like amber. Two objects with the same kind of electric fluid repelled each other, while two objects with different kinds of fluid attracted each other.

What?

By now obsessed, Franklin constructed a simple machine for generating static electricity and got busy electrifying things. An English friend sent him a tube that could produce static electricity, along with an article describing the latest experiments, concluding, somewhat obviously: "Electricity is a vast country, of which we know only some bordering provinces." Using the tube was so much fun that Franklin enlisted a glass-blower and silversmith to make variations on it.

He seldom worked alone, recruiting his friends—other "electricians" (a word he coined). One was Ebenezer Kinnersley, a Baptist minister who lectured on their work up and down the coast, performing tricks Franklin had devised, such as "A flash of lightning made to strike a small house, and dart towards a little lady sitting on a chair."

In the foolhardy tradition of scientists using themselves as guinea pigs, Franklin suffered occasional small shocks while performing his experiments. Once he filled a glass tube with laxative, charged it with electricity, then tried to shock himself with it to see if the laxative would pass into his body. (It didn't.) For the most part, though, he was cautious and never seriously hurt himself.

It became much easier to conduct elaborate electrical experiments with the invention of the Leyden jar in 1745. This was a glass jar filled with water that could be electrified with a wire, which would then store the charge. The jar made it possible to store electricity as long as desired, and then discharge it when you needed it. This was a huge improvement over trying to observe brief shocks of static electricity.

In Leyden, Holland, physicist Peter van Musschen-broek made the accidental discovery of the jar during a "new but terrible experiment," in which he received a severe shock and thought he was about to die. (He didn't.) When he recovered, he started experimenting with his creation.

Franklin got hold of some Leyden jars and started doing his own experiments with them. Some were amusing, like making a metal spider that would jump around. People crowded into his house to giggle at a portrait of England's King George II that would deliver a shock to anyone who touched his crown.

Ben was soon making more significant discoveries. One day while watching the sparks fly from friction and seeing what happened when people tried to trans-fer electricity from one person to another, he realized that the electricity was "not *created* by the friction, but *collected* only." In other words, the experiments were only transferring or redistributing electricity that was already there. This principle is now called the "conser-vation of charge." In fact, the term "charge" was first used by Franklin. Other scientists had been considering the same idea, but Franklin was the first to state it out-right. In physics, conservation of charge later became a crucial concept.

Franklin theorized that "vitreous" and "resinous" electricity were not different types of "electrical fluid" at all, but different forms of the same thing. Electricity was a force that was diffused through all substances, but it was usually in a balanced state. When two ob- jects were rubbed together to collect static electricity, a "positive charge" passed into one object, and a "nega- tive charge" into the other. (Franklin was also the first to label the charges as "positive" and "negative." These are terms we still use today.) The amount of the posi- tive charge was always exactly the same as the amount of the negative charge. When the two objects touched each other, or were connected by something that could conduct electricity, the negative and positive charges would equalize (cancel each other out). The movement of energy as charges equalized was what caused the shock or spark.

This helped explain how the Leyden jar worked. A Leyden jar is made of a substance that is an insu- lator, such as glass—something that doesn't conduct electricity. The inside and outside are covered with a substance that *does* conduct electricity, such as metal. A knob is connected to the inside lining of the jar. The jar must be grounded (that is, connected to the earth by something that can conduct electricity). When you apply an electrical charge to the knob, it is transferred to the inside of the jar. An equal amount of the opposite charge collects on the outside of the jar. The insulating glass prevents the charges from connecting and creating a shock. When the two charges are connected, an electrical current is produced. This is how van Musschenbroek almost shocked himself to death while inventing the jar. He accidentally connected the inner and outer charges with his own body, causing the electric current to run through him.

One important thing Franklin proved was that the electricity in a Leyden jar was located entirely in the insulating material (the glass) and not in the conducting material (the metal coating).

With his experiments, Franklin was treating what had previously been viewed as a special-effects wonder as real science. He was seeing electricity as a powerful part of nature, alongside such other basic forces as gravity, heat, light, and motion. He was among the first to study electricity scientifically.

Along the way, Franklin made many improvements to the Leyden jar that helped the work of other scientists. Van Musschenbroek wrote that "nobody has discovered more recondite mysteries of electricity than

Franklin." He urged Franklin to continue his work: "Then you shall certainly find many other things which have been hidden to natural philosophers throughout the space of centuries."

Through clear and eloquent letters to the best and brightest, especially in Europe, Franklin supplied in-formation about his work, suggested experiments, and asked for feedback. Never dogmatic, he used language rare in his day—"I suggest," "I apprehend"—and he willingly accepted challenges, even offering equipment to those whose views opposed his own. His quest was for truth, not feeding his ego.

It was momentous when his letters were read to England's Royal Society in 1749. The members had railed against articles that were bogged down in "a glo-rious pomp of words." In contrast, here were concise letters presenting a theory of electricity that could pre-dict the outcome of many types of experiments to come. Franklin had rocked the science world.

Two years later, his letters were published in England as an eighty-six-page book, *Experiments and Observations of Electricity*. Written for the average per-son, not for scholars, it was the most widely read sci-ence book of its day. At first, there was no demand for it in America—no printer thought it would sell—but it was translated and published all over Europe.

Scientific fame abroad, however, did help increase Franklin's prestige in America. The same year that his book came out, 1751, he was elected a member of the Pennsylvania Assembly—no longer a mere clerk—and for the next thirty-seven years he would remain in public life, the most effective spokesman America could offer to the world.

In his free time, Franklin never ceased to explore electricity. Once he even threw an "electric picnic" with his fellow electricians. Every aspect of the gathering had to do with the new force of nature. They electrocuted a turkey, then roasted it over a fire made with an electric device (the turkey was "uncommonly tender," he raved). They drank wine in electrified containers that slightly shocked the lips. They ran some electricity across the river to ignite bottles of alcohol on the other side—showing how an electrical charge could operate at a distance.

What a laugh! Or did he guess that someday we'd be cooking with it?

CHAPTER SIX

Lightning Strikes

*E*LECTRICITY QUITE naturally led Franklin to contemplate the bizarre, endlessly fascinating phenomenon of lightning. Neon-yellow jagged streaks piercing the sky had inspired one of his first electrical stunts, "A flash of lightning made to strike a small house."

By 1749 he was wondering "if the fire of electricity and that of lightning be the same." He made a list of twelve things they had in common, such as "being conducted by metals" and "crack or noise on exploding." So what was lightning?

At the time, most people feared lightning, seeing it as a supernatural force. It could kill people instantly, and sparked fires that destroyed houses or burned down entire towns. It was so haphazard, so unpredictable, in what it hit or missed.

Franklin wasn't fearful, though; he was fascinated.

He applied his new knowledge about electricity to the problem of lightning. His theory was that clouds contained water vapors that were electrically charged. He knew from his experiments with Leyden jars that something with a strong electrical charge could discharge without actually touching something else. The charge could pass through the air at a distance from one object to another, creating a visible spark and a cracking noise. Lightning! A really strong charge could go great distances. So he speculated that when "electrified clouds pass over" the land, anything that was sticking up, like tall buildings or trees or hills, could "draw the electrical fire and the whole cloud discharges." The result would be an arc of electricity (the lightning) and a loud crack (the thunder). Lightning, in other words, was nature's way of restoring electrical balance to the atmosphere.

Franklin was not the first scientist to wonder if lightning and electricity were one and the same, but he became the first to design experiments that would prove it. He wasn't confident about his experiments, afraid they might seem too silly and "whimsical." By this point in his career, with a political reputation to protect, he couldn't afford to be laughed at. In a letter, he described his goal. What he needed to do was get lightning to strike a tall rod that was insulated so there'd be no way to get rid of any of the electrical charge. In other words, if lightning was really electricity, the rod should remain full of the electric charge. Then he could check by seeing if it would charge a Leyden jar, or if it produced sparks when touched. Franklin described one possible scenario in a letter in 1750, translated into French two years later. The experiment made use of a specially constructed box protected from rain, the type designed for a sentry on duty, but with a stand inside holding a pointed metal rod that rose some twenty feet above the box. On the top of a tall tower someone inside this sentry box would be next to the stand to observe whether the rod drew off the electrical charge during a storm. If lightning really was electricity, when it struck the rod, the charge would pass into the man. However, if the sentry box had an insulated floor, the electrical charge wouldn't be able to pass out of the man into the earth. This would prevent

the person from being electrocuted. If the floor was not completely insulated, the charge would pass right through the man and probably kill him. If the experiment worked, the man would live but someone could draw electrical sparks from him.

Unfortunately, no buildings in Philadelphia were tall enough for Ben to perform the experiment himself. He would have to wait until Christ Church's steeple was completed, which wasn't going to happen for another four years.

But he could fly a kite, and his second experiment made use of one of his favorite childhood toys. Curiosity had once driven him to follow a tornado on horseback to observe it—for miles. Now curiosity drove him to another potentially fatal action—flying a kite in a storm in order to collect the electric charge from a storm cloud.

With his twenty-one-year-old son William helping, Franklin conducted his famous kite experiment, most probably in 1752. In a storm, out of sight of people who might have considered him crazy, he flew a kite. We don't know exactly how Franklin protected himself from being electrocuted. Probably he relied on his knowledge that dry silk string did not conduct electricity. (Wet string would.) So Franklin had a kite with a silk string, and a key was attached near the bottom of it. Apparently he flew the kite from inside a cow shed, holding on to the dry silk string below the key. When lightning struck the kite, the charge would travel down the wet, rain-soaked string to the key, but would not travel any farther down the dry string.

If lightning really was electricity, then the key would become electrified. One could check whether this had happened by seeing if the key would charge a Leyden jar. Or you could check using your hand, if you didn't mind getting a shock. As Franklin later wrote: "When rain has wet the kite twine so that it can conduct the electric fire freely, you will find it streams out plentifully from the key at the approach of your knuckle." Further experiments could be "performed which are usually done by the help of a rubber glass globe or tube; and therefore the sameness of the electrical matter with that of lightning completely demonstrated."

The amazing experiment proved his theory. Presto—lightning *was* electricity.

Franklin flying his kite in a storm is among the most famous images in American history. Some depictions are inaccurate—for example, those that show William as a little boy, or Ben as an old man. Some people wonder if Franklin actually performed the experiment. He was uncharacteristically vague about the details and never recorded the exact date. The results were not written up for another thirteen years, until Joseph Priestley's *The History and Present State of Electricity* came out in 1767.

But Franklin always claimed to have carried out the experiment, and William never spoke up to contra-dict him. Possibly Franklin wanted to wait to record it until he could do it a second time successfully, aware that his scientific reputation was at stake.

Also, soon after he performed the kite experiment, he learned that the sentry-box experiment had fas-cinated the French King Louis XV so much that he arranged for a performance of it. In May 1752, the ex-periment was carried out successfully, and the king sent a message of thanks to Franklin. So at that point, it was no longer strictly necessary for Ben to repeat the kite experiment. Independently, the French had verified his theory. Was it worth possible ridicule to publicize his kite flying just yet?

Ever practical, Franklin started thinking how this new knowledge could apply to everyday life. He started experimenting with how to best draw off an electrical charge so that it might be controlled. This was a brand-new way of thinking about electricity.

He found that small iron balls didn't draw off the charge nearly as well as pointed pieces of metal. The point had to be sharp, and what worked best of all was an iron bodkin, the type of long needle used by leather-workers.

In 1753, at age forty-six, Franklin invented the lightning rod. It was a simple metal device designed to protect houses and tall buildings by diverting the light-ning into the ground. Fastened to the side of a building with iron staples, the device had "upright rods of iron, made sharp as a needle and gilt to prevent rusting." Once it extracted the electrical charge from a cloud, the rod sent it safely into the earth by way of a wire run-ning down the outside of the building into the ground.

Ben's invention showed his mastery of the concept of electrical grounding—the fact that even a strong electrical charge could be neutralized by conducting it into the earth—and his understanding of the way some things conduct electricity and some don't. Metal conducted, dry wood didn't. That's why lightning was so haphazard. The important detail about his lightning rod is that it had to be grounded, connected to the earth by something that conducted electricity. So the lightning rod was the opposite of the rod in his sentry-box experiment—since the rod in the sentry box was not grounded, the charge remained stored in the rod.

As with the stove, Franklin could have patented his lightning-rod invention and made money. Instead he put directions for its construction in the *Almanack*—in between notices of Quaker meetings and court dates—so that anyone could have one.

The invention, clearly designed to save lives and property, was more controversial than you'd think. Popular belief held that lightning was an act of God, or Satan. If it was God's will that your house burned down, it was morally wrong to interfere.

One widely held belief was that ringing church bells during storms would scare the lightning away, dispel its evil energy. Even the philosopher René Descartes believed that bell-ringing worked. Ironically, many churches and many bell-ringers were struck by lightning—the metal bells, located high up in steeples, were *attracting* the lightning, not repelling it. The bell tower at St. Mark's in Venice was hit nine times by lightning before a rod was installed in 1766—and after that it was never hit again.

Franklin's closest rival in electricity studies was Abbé Nollet, the court scientist at the time to the

French king. Abbé Nollet totally rejected the rod for religious reasons: "It is as impious to ward off God's lightnings as for a child to resist the chastening rod of the father."

Lightning was actually a bigger problem in Europe than in America; because churches there often stored gunpowder, lightning strikes created terrible explosions. But Europe was slow to adopt the rods. In some villages people tore them down after their installation. Even in America, some religious people blamed lightning rods for "causing" earthquakes by forcing lightning into the earth.

Franklin went ahead and rigged up his own house with a rod, with two loud bells that would ring when it was active. Deborah found it quite annoying.

For the rest of his life Franklin kept track of all the rods that were eventually installed in America, proudly noticing how each building no longer suffered the "mischievous effects" of lightning.

England's Royal Society made him the first American to win its Copley Medal in 1753 for "his curious experiments and observations on electricity." Three years later he became one of the few Americans elected a Fellow of the Royal Society. Joseph Priestley, the English scientist who later discovered oxygen, often compared Franklin's pioneering work to Franklin's hero—"the greatest, perhaps, that has been made in the whole compass of philosophy, since the time of Sir Isaac Newton."

Even better than the acclaim was the enormous satisfaction of knowing his discovery made a difference in the lives of so many people. The lightning rod was no small accomplishment—it was a stunning example of the way that an understanding of science could control natural forces and make everyday life safer.

CHAPTER SEVEN

And More

WITH PHILADELPHIA on its way to becoming America's leading city, Franklin was its genius-in-residence. Anyone who had a bright idea or project came to see him first.

In his journal, Ben began each day by writing, "What good shall I do this day?" Each night he ended by writing, "What good have I done today?"

While doing good for America, he kept trying to make himself useful in science. And so he theorized about and explored myriad subjects.

As befit his interest in health, many of his brainstorms were medical in nature. After his brother (John, not the tyrannical James) fell ill and requested a skinny tube that would help him urinate with less pain, Franklin invented the first flexible urinary catheter in America. He was the first to diagnose lead poison-ing, a potentially fatal condition. He had noticed how badly his hands ached after handling hot lead type for printing. Then he noticed how many people in various occupations—printers, plumbers, painters—fell ill or sometimes lost the use of their hands. He connected the dots, identifying working with lead as the common factor among a wide range of ailments. His stoves, he always emphasized, were made of iron, not lead.

Sick people often came to him, and, a bit reluc-tantly, he agreed to treat them, employing electric shock therapy when he thought it might work. With stroke victims or those suffering other types of paraly-sis, Franklin had some small successes in restoring move-ment with electric shocks. But the effect never seemed to last, and at times he believed the patients felt better merely from coming to see him and getting some treat-ment. Franklin's intuition about the curative power of electricity was right, of course. Electric shock treatment is still used today to treat severe depression; pacemakers implanted in patients with heart disease can give an electric shock that restores normal heart rhythm in a potentially fatal situation.

Franklin was among the first to recommend citrus fruit to prevent scurvy, which started with bleeding gums and loss of teeth and could eventually lead to death. Not until 1932 was there proof that scurvy was caused by a deficiency in vitamin C, which citrus fruit supplies. Meanwhile, also interested in refrigeration, Franklin urged keeping food as fresh as possible to cut down on food poisoning.

He was big on fresh air and clean hands. Years before germ theory was discovered in the 1870s by Louis Pasteur (who educated himself by reading Franklin's book on electricity), Franklin postulated that tiny particles could enter a vulnerable body and cause disease. He started to compile notes for a whole treatise about contagion and how to prevent colds. He never finished it, but he shared his thoughts with friends.

He was so keen on health, he had helped to establish Pennsylvania Hospital in 1751—the first hospital in America. Until then, poor people who couldn't take care of themselves were dumped at workhouses, getting no medical attention, and the mentally ill were often homeless. With twenty beds and just one doctor at first, the new hospital was open to all, rich or poor, treating both mental and physical illnesses. It fed patients healthy meals with vegetables, along with wine, beer, and rum, which were believed to be helpful in regaining health.

A huge fan of exercise, Franklin believed it could prevent various diseases. And he was also one of the first to work out—in today's language—as a means of burning calories and keeping in shape. He believed schools should provide several hours of exercise every day and that physical activity was just as important for girls as boys.

A very early ecologist, he was upset about the dirty air in cities—he was appalled at how smoky and polluted London was, for example. He found he needed to go miles into the country to get a breath of fresh air. Besides tinkering with his stove, he wrote long papers about how to solve the problem of belching chimneys.

A problem of aging was poorer eyesight. Franklin appreciated the theories of vision presented in Newton's *Opticks*. As he aged, he wearied of switching between the spectacles he needed for close work and the pair he needed to see things far away. One day he got a glass cutter to saw both pairs in half, and then he reassembled them with glue so that the bottom half of each lens was for near vision, the top half was for far. "Most convenient," he raved about his new bifocal glasses, and millions went on to copy him.

He performed experiments to show the amount of heat that different colors absorbed from the sun. As always, the work had a practical purpose. Franklin advised people that they'd feel cooler and more comfortable by wearing white or light colors on hot sunny days because light colors absorbed less heat.

A lover of music—he enjoyed singing, composed music, and played several instruments—he invented a new glass instrument called the armonica (not to be confused with the metal harmonica). Inspired by a con-

cert performed with wet fingers on wineglasses, he constructed his armonica with thirty-seven glass bowls of different sizes arranged on a spinning rod. The player set the bowls into motion with foot pedals and then touched their rims with a wet finger. The sound was eerie, otherworldly. Mozart and Beethoven wrote music for it, and it remained popular for forty years. Franklin always claimed this as the favorite of all his inventions.

From a total of eight transatlantic voyages, he became intensely interested in the flow of water. Was there a way it could move ships faster? After discussions with sailors, he was the first to chart the path of a warm current flowing clockwise through the Atlantic from the Gulf of Florida. He labeled it the Gulf Stream. To determine the boundaries of the warmer waters of the stream he invented a thermometer that could measure temperatures at depths below one hundred feet.

It took years for British sea captains to use his advice on navigating the Gulf Stream, but eventually they realized it shaved two weeks off the sailing time from London to America's port cities. Later scientists refined Franklin's work, but his measurements are similar to what satellites measure today, and we still call this current the Gulf Stream.

On his voyages he kept noticing that even in rough

water the seas behind the ship were weirdly still. He finally noticed the cooks emptying their oily cooking water behind them. He observed how oil always floated on top of water, calming the waves. He enjoyed showing off this factoid to friends, designing a cane with oil at its tip so he could appear to calm waters by magic.

Trying to observe a lunar eclipse on a Friday in 1743, Franklin grew annoyed when a storm wrecked his view by surging into Philadelphia from the northeast. Even though Boston is to the northeast of Philadelphia, Bostonians had been able to see the eclipse because the same storm had not reached Boston until Saturday. Franklin discovered that the storm had actually moved up the Atlantic coast, rather than moving into Pennsylvania from the north. So he theorized that storms don't necessarily move in the direction of their prevailing wind, as everyone had previously believed. This and other of his weather ideas helped establish the science of meteorology.

Experimenting to figure out why ants could always find their way into his jar of molasses, he deduced that ants communicate with one another in some way—years before scientists confirmed it.

People brought him fossils to evaluate, fossils that came from what Franklin called "ancient elephants from before the flood." Paleontology was in its earliest days, but Franklin, way ahead of his time, accepted the idea of extinction and considered that climate changes may have killed off some prehistoric animals. His American Philosophical Society would later play an important role in the study of fossils.

Delighted by the quick growth of the American population, he made predictions and gave formulas. For example, he calculated that the American population, doubling every twenty years, even without new immigrants, would outnumber England's within one hundred years. He was correct, and this was the birth of demographic study.

Franklin designed new streetlamps for Philadelphia that gave off much more light than ones he'd seen in London. London's lamps had no vent for dirty air to escape, so the trapped smoke eventually darkened the glass. Franklin's lamps had vents, plus a chimney, and he didn't use a glass globe, but rather four separate panes of glass, so lamps would be easier to fix. His city's streets were known as the brightest in the world. And they were also the easiest to travel on—Franklin was the leader in getting Philadelphia's streets paved with cobblestones.

He worked with one of America's evangelical ministers to build a great hall to host speakers from any religion, including Islam. He donated money to every single church and synagogue in Philadelphia. He also played a starring role in establishing the first non-religious college in America, what came to be known as the University of Pennsylvania. He helped to shape its curriculum, which emphasized science—all men, no matter what their future careers, should have an understanding of natural laws—plus practical information on agriculture, health, diet, and, of course, how to swim. (Harvard and Yale, by comparison, were founded primarily to educate young men for the ministry.)

Then he helped add America's first medical school to the college in 1765. It graduated its first class of forty students two years later. (Before this, Franklin had made do by helping the brightest boys he knew to get into medical school in Scotland.)

Whew. Small wonder that Franklin, with his mere two years of formal schooling, went on to receive honorary degrees from four of America's colleges, as well as honorary doctorates from universities in Europe.

His honorary degrees earned him the right to be known as "Dr. Franklin"—and he treasured it. But the biggest reward, he felt, as always, was being useful.

CHAPTER EIGHT

Wrong Turns, Right Turns, and Funny Turns

BEN FRANKLIN COULD be silly, but even his silliness had scientific overtones. Interested in all things coming out of a body, for example, he once wrote a funny essay about farts: "What comfort can the vortices of Descartes give to a man who has whirlwinds in his bowels! The knowledge of Newton's mutual *attraction* of the particles of matter, can it afford ease to him who is racked by their mutual *repulsion*, and the cruel distensions it occasions?" He called for something that "shall render the natural discharges of wind from our bodies, not only inoffensive, but agreeable as perfumes." No one followed up on this.

Another treatment that never caught on was "air baths." He personally spent an hour or so of each day nude with the window open, believing that airing the body kept one healthy. Few, if any, copied him.

And then there was Franklin's portable bathtub. As he got too old for swimming, he invented a tub he could travel with, one with a lid that covered everything except his head. He could soak in hot water while chatting with visitors.

He had an unusual interest in perspiration and the ways it evaporated, especially at night. People who could afford it should have two beds, he advised, getting into the cool one when the other got hot. Otherwise, you should use your arm and leg to lift the blankets to let in air—repeat this twenty times before trying to fall asleep again.

A man of his times in many ways, Franklin made some wrong turns and held attitudes that we consider offensive. He professed a dislike of whole groups of people, such as the Germans who were moving to Pennsylvania. His view of American Indians was mixed. He admired their survival skills in the wilderness and spoke out against cruelty to them, but believed they were inferior to white people and that they would eventually disappear.

And he owned African slaves for thirty years—
Peter and Jemima, later a boy named Othello, and then
a fourth, named George, accepted as payment for a debt.

On the question of slavery, Franklin's open, ques-
tioning mind eventually changed. Possibly prompted by
Deborah, he visited schools for black children, who he
admitted are "in every respect equal to white children."
He decided slavery was an "atrocious abasement of human nature," freed his slaves, and toward the end of his
life, wrote several essays arguing for the education of
blacks and their integration into American society. He
eventually became president of the Pennsylvania Abolition Society, the first such organization in the New
World, prompting his state to abolish slavery, in 1780.
He even petitioned Congress to abolish slavery in every
state—a proposal that was quickly rejected. One South-
ern representative called Franklin senile, and another predicted, "This would never be submitted to by the South-
ern states without a civil war." (It would take another
seventy-five years and the Civil War before Congress
finally abolished slavery.)

He was also poised to revise his negative attitude
toward women's education.

During his stays in London, Franklin became

friends with his landlady, Margaret Stevenson, and her lively daughter Polly. Charmed by Polly's obviously bright mind, Franklin encouraged her further education. This was a marked change from his attitude toward the schooling of his own daughter, Sally. He saw that she knew the basics of reading and writing, but emphasized that her needlework was more important. Later Franklin wrote Polly long letters about electricity and such matters as how the moon affects the tides and how barometers work. Eight of these letters to Polly had such precise explanations of electricity that they were eventually included in his revised book on the subject.

All the while, through wrong turns, right turns, and dead ends, Deborah kept him fed with bread and milk for breakfast and all-American meals of hams she cured herself, dried venison, salted fish, local apples, ground maize, and cranberries. They lived in a series of rented houses until Ben built a comfortable brick house on Market Street, with what might have been the first indoor plumbing in the Colonies.

The whole second floor was Franklin's library, which eventually boasted almost 4,300 books, plus unusual medical equipment. The third floor, devoted

to music, housed his instruments. This was where he
played duets with Sally.

Franklin was obsessed with every last detail of
his house's construction, down to the hinges and door-
knobs and the exact color of each room.

One of history's mysteries is: where did Franklin
find the time for such details while his political life was
heating to a boil?

CHAPTER NINE

In His Spare Time

SO ADMIRED IN ENGLAND, Franklin found his stature rising in the Colonies, too. As of 1757, the Pennsylvania Assembly sent him to London as its agent, to serve as a colonial "ambassador." Ben spent a total of fifteen years in Great Britain, representing all thirteen colonies, trying to make sure Britain treated them fairly—and yet never abandoning his science.

What about his wife, Deborah? Her fear of the sea—much more common than Ben's love of it—meant that she never joined Franklin on his trips abroad, even though he asked her to. Caught up in socializing with a slew of new friends in politics and science, Ben didn't press Deborah too hard to go with him, perhaps realiz- ing that she wouldn't really fit in with his new crowd. Deborah remained his rock, missing him but dutifully taking care of everything he left behind, with the aid of one or two slaves.

In Franklin's later years, the Colonies needed him like never before. He was simply too talented to be left in peace to pursue scientific endeavors while the politi- cal landscape in America was changing in drastic ways. The pivotal year was 1765, when he was fifty-nine.

At first, serving in Great Britain as a diplomat rep- resenting the American colonies, he was conciliatory and did not always fight the tyrannical treatment doled out by the king and Parliament. But Franklin's ideas changed after 1765. That was the year Britain imposed the Stamp Act, a tax on papers and documents. An extremely unpopular move—"taxation without repre- sentation" was what the statesman and orator Patrick Henry called it. It meant that British government de- cided what taxes were imposed on the Colonies with- out anybody in America having a say in it. Franklin agreed with Patrick Henry and helped to persuade Parliament to repeal the tax the following year. Was it time, he wondered, for the Colonies to declare their independence from Great Britain, this bullying older brother?

While in England, he kept up his science studies as best as he could. Whenever he rented apartments, one room was always for experiments with electricity. For companionship he rode horses with Royal Society members or hung out with them in some of London's five hundred coffeehouses. His best friend was a well-known doctor, Sir John Pringle, and he spent time with his pal Joseph Priestley, discoverer of oxygen.

He visited other scientists such as Erasmus Darwin (Charles Darwin's grandfather) at his home in Lichfield. He joined the influential Lunar Society of Birmingham, making friends with people like Matthew Boulton and James Watt (later to invent the steam engine) and Josiah Wedgwood (Darwin's other grandfather, the famous pottery manufacturer). Wherever he went, Ben installed lightning rods upon request.

Franklin did the math and predicted that America, with its growing population, could one day defeat Britain. But how? As it stood, the Colonies' motley army, without even enough guns to go around, was in no shape to go to war against an empire with the best armed forces in the world. Franklin's ultimate conclusion, though, was that America simply had to separate from Great Britain by any means necessary, including war.

His stance, unfortunately, permanently estranged him from his son William, who had become governor of New Jersey. William remained loyal to the British crown, was later arrested for his beliefs, and eventually moved to England. After 1775, except for one brief encounter, father and son never saw each other again.

He also never saw Deborah during the last ten years of her life. Even after she had a stroke and wrote to him in 1769 attributing her illness to "dissatisfied distress" at his long absence, Franklin stayed in London. She died after another stroke in 1774. "I have lately lost my old and faithful companion," he mourned.

By the time he did return to Philadelphia in 1775, war had broken out. The Boston Tea Party protest had led to fighting at Lexington and Concord, Massachusetts. The American Revolution had begun.

In 1776 in Philadelphia, Ben, twenty to forty years older than the other men involved, was one of the Committee of Five that drafted the Declaration of Independence. Franklin even added a scientific touch to the document when he revised Thomas Jefferson's "We hold these truths to be sacred and undeniable." To Franklin, nature revealed truths for humans to follow, and he changed the phrasing to "We hold these truths to be self-evident." A small thing, but it pointed the document away from religion and toward rationality.

The first public reading of the Declaration took place on a platform that Franklin's American Philo-sophical Society had built years earlier to observe the planet Venus.

But how *did* America defeat one of the world's superpowers? It was Ben Franklin to the rescue.

CHAPTER TEN

Franklinmania

*B*en Franklin immediately assumed various key roles in the Revolution, including loan- ing his own money to the troops and fighting hard to get them inoculated against illness. Ten times as many of General George Washington's soldiers were dying from illnesses like smallpox than from wounds— until he began inoculating his troops. But Franklin's most important contribution was a trip to France.

To win the war, the Americans needed all the help they could get, specifically the support of another superpower—Britain's archenemy, France. At the time, France did not officially recognize the United States as a country. Congress sent Franklin, then entering his seventies, to persuade the French to help America in the war effort.

By this time he was known as the man who had tamed lightning. He'd become internationally famous for his science—the most accomplished man in the world, almost superhuman, even feared. Rumors swirled that he had electrical machines that could move continents and oceans around. It was said that Franklin had deflecting mirrors that, when set up, could burn down the British fleet.

In France, where new ideas in science were all the rage, regardless of whether they were solid or quirky, Franklin was all but worshiped. The French followed his work closely, called electricians *franklinistes*, and were overjoyed to receive him as an American diplomat in 1776.

During two trips, he was to spend a total of nine years there—some of his most colorful as well as scientifically interesting.

His arrival in Paris created a sensation. Shops carried Ben Franklin merchandise—dolls, ashtrays, wallpaper, everything. "These . . . have made your father's face as well known as that of the moon," he wrote to his daughter Sally. Fans hoped for a glimpse of Franklin as he himself had once tried to glimpse Newton, and fashionable ladies created hairdos that resembled his eccentric fur cap, the *coiffure à la Franklin*. (A painful scalp rash had forced him to adopt hats and abandon wearing the customary wig.) Supposedly, he charmed the ladies as easily as he charmed lightning. A widower for several years by this point, he enjoyed the company of witty women and proposed (unsuccessfully) to at least one.

Near the royal laboratory close to Paris, he set up house where he stayed for free in exchange for installing a lightning rod and getting the chimneys fixed.

Thanks to his reputation in science, Franklin was introduced to all the VIPs, including King Louis XVI. Among the fashionable, he was the star of salons.

Abandoning his own rules about moderation, he became a lover of wine and heavy food, calling himself Dr. Fatsides. His wine cellar boasted over a thousand bottles, of which he preferred the rich Madeira.

But the whole time, Franklin was working the rooms with a critical mission foremost in mind. He was using his celebrity to get money, guns, and gunpowder from the French for the American underdogs in the ongoing war with Great Britain.

It was said that political people in France spoke two languages: their native French, and a sort of code for what they *really* meant. Franklin mastered both.

All his life he'd been an avid chess player—"Games lubricate the mind," he said—and in France the games sometimes lasted all night. He claimed that his skill in chess helped his diplomacy: "Life is a kind of chess, in which we have points to gain and competitors or adversaries to contend with." Chess was good for mastering caution, looking ahead several moves, keeping one's cool—things he excelled at.

Within two years, in 1778, he succeeded in formalizing a Franco-American alliance with a treaty that won France's aid without sacrificing American independence—a major diplomatic triumph. France began sending fleets and armies, as well as weapons, to America's aid. He stayed in his position of ambassador to make sure the treaty was observed, to keep the money flowing—and to enjoy France.

He still made time for science. He often dined at the house of Antoine Lavoisier, who was the first to investigate the principles of modern chemistry. Chemistry was the talk of the town, with the isolation of oxygen, and then hydrogen, leading to the discovery in

1783 that when the two of them were combined, they created water.

He met with Alessandro Volta, an Italian scientist who was trying to improve upon the Leyden jar. In 1775 Volta was working on an "electrophore" machine that retained a charge indefinitely—in other words, a primitive battery. Franklin did not have the opportunity to test it himself, but others did.

He also witnessed the spectacular aurora borealis display of 1778. The mysterious phenomenon known as the Northern Lights had always fascinated him, and he took four days off from his diplomatic maneuverings to write up his observations, complete with diagrams, about what caused the Northern Lights. Probably an electrical event in the atmosphere, he theorized (a theory that was proven correct in 1900).

Few people were giddier than Franklin at the reports of a new French flying machine, the biggest deal of the age. Since first seeing birds, people had dreamed of ascending to the skies, although without any success until now.

Two brothers, the Montgolfiers, inspired by seeing a piece of cloth lifted into the air by the heat from a fireplace, made a silk balloon and pumped heated air into it. Along with hundreds of thousands of others, Franklin breathlessly watched all the first balloon flights in 1783—unmanned, manned, with animals (a rooster, sheep, and duck), and using hydrogen gas instead of hot air. "Never before was a philosophical experiment so magnificently attended," said Franklin of the record-breaking crowds. While women fainted, he cheered.

Some thought these balloons were the devil's work and found them terrifying, like witches riding a broom; sometimes farmers attacked and destroyed a balloon as it landed. As for the English, most of them had no use for what the Royal Society called French "ballomania."

But Franklin, when he overheard a skeptic complain, "What's the use of a balloon?" retorted, "What's the *use* of a newborn baby?"

Franklin realized the immense significance of these experiments, all the possibilities they opened up, paving "the way to some discoveries in natural philosophy of which at present we have no conception." He immediately dreamed up practical uses—balloons could carry foods to places faster and to higher elevations, where the colder air could keep foods fresher, slowing spoilage that caused food poisoning. They could be used to transport disabled people without inflicting pain. And, close to his heart, they could be labs in the air for up-close study of electricity in clouds.

Soon balloons were floating all over France. Franklin knew all the balloonists, helped to fund their flights, and laughed with them as they described the experience of flying as "total hilarity."

This was a moment when he wished he could be alive a thousand years into the future: "The rapid progress *true* science now makes occasions my regretting sometimes I was born so soon."

The French, however, sometimes rushed to take up fads that were dressed up as science but in reality were just hokum. One such craze of the time was "mesmerism," named for German healer Franz Mesmer. Mesmer theorized that heavenly bodies emitted a universal fluid, an "animal magnetism" that could become blocked within a human body—blockages that only he could cure. He staged theatrical events where he played eerie music on an armonica (the instrument invented by Franklin); wore robes of lilac; and used special lighting, mirrors, and a wand to cure just about anything with his "magnetic fluid." At the height of his popularity, in 1784, he was treating a hundred patients a day, including members of the royal family, and making piles of money.

Some women were starting to complain about being taken advantage of while under Mesmer's spell. The whole thing sounded fishy to Franklin.

He became co-chairman of a commission to check out whether Mesmer was a quack. It may have been the first investigation of scientific fraud in history, and Franklin was on the case, along with Lavoisier, the astronomer Jean-Sylvain Bailly, and the doctor Joseph-Ignace Guillotin, who would later give his name to the supposedly pain-free machine used to behead so many people during France's very bloody revolution of 1789.

In a series of elegant, controlled experiments—for example, blindfolding patients to see whether they could find a tree infused with animal magnetism (they couldn't)—the group debunked Mesmer as a fake and "magnetic fluid" as nonexistent. They reported that Mesmer's patients were "cured" because they believed they would be—it was possibly the first mention of what we now call the placebo or "sugar pill" effect. As Franklin noted, "There is a wonderful deal of credulity in the world, and deceptions as absurd have supported themselves for ages."

Mesmer left town, leaving behind the verb "mesmerize" which means to fascinate or put under a spell.

Franklin's last visitor in France was a Dutch elec-
trician and huge fan, Martinus van Marum, who had
designed the largest electrical friction machine in the
world. He had succeeded in getting his machine to
make a printed impression of an electrical charge traveling from a positive conductor to a negative one. It
clearly showed one flow going in one direction, not
two fluids going in opposite directions. Elated at this
image, the elderly Franklin said, "This then proves my
theory of a single electrical fluid, and it is now high
time to reject the theory of two sorts of fluids."

Though Franklin had already succeeded in secur-
ing a formal alliance with France, he was considered so
valuable that the U.S. Congress wanted him to stay on
as their ambassador to maintain the crucial relationship.

Franklin finally left France at age seventy-nine,
even more of a superstar than when he arrived—and
an all-out hero to Americans. France's naval and military strength had been vital to victory in the American Revolution. Franklin had gotten the help that made
independence possible.

CHAPTER ELEVEN

Under the Mulberry Tree

*W*ITH THE FIGHTING in America over, and as much as he loved France, Franklin itched to get home to Philadelphia and "peaceful times." He urged a science friend to come visit him, promising, "We will make plenty of experiments together." But bouts with illness and his continuing work as ambassador delayed his return.

On his voyage home in 1785, Franklin indulged his passion for natural phenomena. He happily scribbled forty pages of observations about the sea, with charts, instructions on building better boats, a comparative study of all seaworthy vessels in the world, and more on the Gulf Stream. He gathered his latest ideas in *Sundry Maritime Observations*, which he published the following year. It proposed new anchors, watertight sections, and shipboard lightning rods, plus a soup bowl that stayed stable during storms.

His two tons of luggage included a disassembled printing machine, twenty-three crates of books, one crate of fruit trees, three Angora cats, and four boxes of scientific equipment.

As his ship pulled into Philadelphia, now the capital of the United States of America, church bells chimed and a huge, cheering crowd greeted him. This homecoming was in stark contrast to his first arrival in the city as a forlorn seventeen-year-old. Franklin had become a champion of American independence, alongside George Washington, Thomas Jefferson, and others a generation younger than Franklin was.

Back in his comfortable house, he was thrilled to see his lightning rod with its tip melted—meaning that lightning had struck without harming the structure. Sally, who had married and had seven children, cared for her father as well.

He had fun showing visitors his equipment and experiments, as well as his prized possession, a large preserved two-headed snake he'd been given.

But if Franklin imagined that he'd be left alone to pursue his scientific interests, he was wrong. The country was too new to do without his guidance. Franklin said, resentfully, "They have eaten my flesh, and seem resolved now to pick my bones."

During the Constitutional Convention of 1787, the eighty-one-year-old Franklin organized weekly meetings at his house to investigate the "science of government" and how to structure it. Should America remain thirteen independent states or form one nation? Why not both, he put forth in a compromise—and got all to agree.

He did long calculations showing how smaller states could have as much power as larger ones with his vision of a single-chambered Congress. Then, after those who supported a Congress of two parts—the Senate and the House of Representatives—won their argument, open-minded as ever, he supported them.

Establishing a democracy was to him like a science project. Passionate about progress in science, he pinned his hopes on similar progress in human behavior: "O that moral science were in as fair a way of improvement, that men would cease to be wolves to one another, and that human beings would at length learn what they now improperly call humanity!"

The aspect of the new American Constitution that pleased him the most? That it could be changed by amendment to take into account future developments, just as scientific theories change when new and better data comes in.

Franklin spent his last couple of years sheltering the other Founding Fathers under the shade of the mulberry tree in his garden, still speculating about science.

He tried to stay in shape with walking, swimming, and lifting weights.

But gradually his health failed, his chief ailment being gout, a painful swelling of the joints. He took a medicine derived from the saffron plant. He also scoured the most recent medical book on gout and tried to follow its advice for eating and drinking more moderately, relieved that the book dispensed with older remedies like applying ox poop wrapped in cabbage leaves, or eating a roast goose stuffed with lard, wax, and chopped-up kittens.

He had few teeth left; he also suffered from an excruciating kidney stone so large he could feel it when he turned over in bed. He rejected pain relievers as long as he could, then finally resorted to opium and alcohol.

His last letter was to Thomas Jefferson, the new

Secretary of State, and was all about maps of the western boundaries to their new country.

Surrounded by family, Franklin died on April 17, 1790, at the ripe old age of eighty-four. He bequeathed most of his money to his family (except William), with large sums each to the cities of Boston and Philadelphia.

Intrigued by all aspects of life, Franklin had once fantasized about the perfect death, hoping that he could be preserved until the day science figured out how to bring him back to life: "Being immersed with a few friends in a cask of Madeira, until that time, then to be recalled to life by the solar warmth of my dear country!" More realistically, he added, "But in all probability, we live in a century too little advanced, and too near the infancy of science, to see such an art brought in our time to its perfection."

He wasn't able to manage his temporary immersion in wine—no one has so far—but the outpouring of affection after his death would have warmed his heart.

In America he was cheered as a patriot, while France was more apt to see him in dual roles—a patriot and a scientist. France declared its first-ever state of national mourning upon his death; for three days French citizens wore black. At his Paris memorial service, he was compared to the ancient Greek Pythagoras, the groundbreaking philosopher and mathematician, for using the "laws of nature" to discover truth.

Back in Philadelphia, approximately twenty thousand people attended his funeral, the largest crowd thus far in the city. People of all religions and all the city's printers were represented, as well as members of the organizations and schools Franklin had helped found. Also present were citizens inoculated against smallpox, people who took better care of themselves as *Poor Richard* had advised, those whose lives had been saved by lightning rods, and Americans from all walks of life who knew a lot more about science thanks to him.

CHAPTER TWELVE

Lasting Impact

THE POWER OF electricity changed the world, and Franklin was there to light the spark. He moved the study of electricity a giant step forward, and it became established as a science.

But in America, his earliest biographers, like most people, lacked scientific training and tended to overlook his accomplishments in that area. Even by 1938, in an eight-hundred-page biography of Franklin, only one brief chapter was devoted to science. He was portrayed as a hero, a patriot, a guy who flew a kite, but not a gifted scientist. The word "scientist," after all, was not coined until 1833—that's how far Franklin was ahead of his time.

Even by the twentieth century, there were more foreign editions of Franklin's scientific studies than American ones. In fact, his masterpiece, *Experiments and Observations of Electricity*, was not printed in the United States until 1941.

Yet being American was actually part of Franklin's genius—he was self-taught, an outsider, a pioneer who saw things in a way that those in the Old World didn't.

Franklin himself has become part of our culture, a familiar icon. Among many other people, two of our presidents (Franklin Pierce and Franklin Roosevelt) were named for him. The city of Philadelphia alone has about five thousand likenesses of Franklin, and anyone who has a hundred-dollar bill knows why it's called a Benjamin.

American and European scientists built on his work. As he himself noted, "Even short hints and imperfect experiments in any new branch of science, being communicated, have oftentimes a good effect, in exciting the attention of the ingenious." He understood that future scientists, by standing on his shoulders, would make discoveries that he had not. It was more important to increase knowledge than to inflate his own ego or bank account. Always he gave away his knowledge freely.

Over time, lightning rods came to be mass produced in factories instead of being individually made by blacksmiths. As late as the 1830s the lightning rod was still viewed as the best example of how science improves people's everyday lives. Other practical inventions have taken its place, but buildings without lightning rods continue to be hit by lightning and burn down.

He was the role model for all kinds of scientists. English manufacturer Matthew Boulton (inspired by experimenting with Franklin on the Leyden jar) and Scottish engineer James Watt, fellow members of the Lunar Society, went on to change the world: They invented an engine fueled by steam, manufacturing 450 of them by 1800. Steam engines powered new factories, then tractors, trains, and boats. The Industrial Age was dawning.

British chemist Humphry Davy used Franklin's work, applying electric current to substances to observe the reactions. In the process he discovered potassium in 1807, followed by sodium, calcium, and other new elements.

In 1800, Italian scientist Alessandro Volta finally succeeded in inventing a working battery. Layering copper and zinc, he invented a much steadier source of electrical energy than the Leyden jar or anything else so far. Now electricity could be measured in standard units, which were named volts in Volta's honor.

Once, Franklin's electrical picnickers had sent an electric current across a river. But in fact that current could travel much longer distances. Thanks in part to work by American inventor Samuel Morse, electric cable was submerged in the ocean in 1844 to transmit a telegraph message. Electricity led to faster and faster forms of communication, connecting the world.

In the field of physics, men such as English scientist Michael Faraday (inventor of the first electric motor in 1821), and later on Scottish scientist James Clerk Maxwell with his 1864 theory of electromagnetism, made major breakthroughs in the understanding of electricity.

American scientist Thomas Edison came on the scene with one fabulous invention after another, including the electric phonograph to play music in 1877, then the first practical electric lightbulb in 1879, and about twenty years later a device to capture moving images and project them as motion pictures—movies.

These days we have endless ways of exploiting electricity as a source of energy—computers, lighting, heat, transportation, entertainment . . . It permeates every aspect of life, making it safer and happier, just as Franklin would have liked.

Franklin's influence is everywhere. By establishing electricity as a flow of particles, for example, he influenced particle physics. Some would even like to credit Franklin for discovering the elementary particle known as the electron instead of British physicist J. J. Thomson, who won the Nobel Prize for the discovery in 1906.

As for lightning, the first photograph of it was taken around 1885, and the first measurements of its electricity were made in 1897. We now know that it can be charged with millions of volts of electricity and can reach a temperature of more than 50,000 degrees Fahrenheit—five times as hot as the surface of the sun. Tampa Bay, Florida, is known as the lightning capital of North America—21,000 flashes of it in one month in 1993 alone. In 2010 a camera was invented that took the first X-ray images of lightning striking in Florida. We're still learning more about lightning. One current theory is that it sparked life on earth, jump-starting chemical evolution.

Were he alive today, Franklin might be working on climate change. The Gulf Stream he observed may be threatened by global warming; scientists are concerned for its very existence. Or he'd be traveling in space, curing cancer, designing robots, or doing all of these at the same time while starting up the latest high-tech business, handling social media with style and verve, and urging everyone else on.

Franklin himself once summed up his mission in a few words after a near-death experience. He had just barely escaped a midnight shipwreck, and he quipped that a religious man might, in gratitude, have built a chapel on the spot.

He, however, was more inclined to build a lighthouse.

Light, more light.

SOURCES

(*especially for young readers)

BOOKS

*Barretta, Gene. *Now and Ben: The Modern Inventions of Ben Franklin.* New York: Holt, 2006.

Chaplin, Joyce E. *The First Scientific American: Benjamin Franklin and the Pursuit of Genius.* New York: Perseus, 2006.

Cohen, Bernard I. *Benjamin Franklin's Science.* Cambridge: Harvard University Press, 1990.

———. *Science and the Founding Fathers: Science in the Political Thought of Thomas Jefferson, Benjamin Franklin, John Adams, and James Madison.* New York: Norton, 1995.

Dray, Philip. *Stealing God's Thunder: Benjamin Franklin's Lightning Rod and the Invention of America.* New York: Random House, 2005.

Finger, Stanley. *Doctor Franklin's Medicine.* Philadelphia: University of Pennsylvania Press, 2006.

*Fleming, Candace. *Ben Franklin's Almanac: Being a True Account of the Good Gentleman's Life.* New York: Atheneum, 2003.

Franklin, Benjamin. *The Autobiography and Other Writings*, edited by Kenneth Silverman. New York: Penguin, 1986.

*Giblin, James Cross. *The Amazing Life of Benjamin Franklin*. New York: Scholastic, 2000.

Isaacson, Walter. *Benjamin Franklin: An American Life*. New York: Simon & Schuster, 2003.

*Schroeder, Alan. *Ben Franklin: His Wit and Wisdom from A–Z*. New York: Holiday House, 2011.

Tanford, Charles. *Ben Franklin Stilled the Waves: An Informal History of Pouring Oil on Water with Reflections on the Ups and Downs of Scientific Life in General*. New York: Oxford University Press, 2004.

WEBSITES

American Philosophical Society: http://www.amphilsoc.org

Autobiography of Benjamin Franklin:
http://www.earlyamerica.com/lives/franklin

Ben Franklin: In Search of a Better World:
http://www.benfranklin300.org

The Electric Ben Franklin:
http://www.ushistory.org/franklin/index.htm

Library Company of Philadelphia: http://www.librarycompany.org

INDEX

Note: Page numbers in *italics* indicate illustrations.

abolitionism, 82

Account of the New Invented Pennsylvanian Fire-Places (Franklin), 46

aether theory, 51–52

air baths, 80

air pollution, 73

alcohol use, 73, 92, 102–3

ambassadorship of Franklin, 90–98

ambition of Franklin, 32–39

amendments to the Constitution, 102

American Indians, 80

American Philosophical Society, 37–38, 77, 89

American Revolution, 88–89, 90–98, *99*

"animal magnetism," 96–98

apprenticeships, 22, 28

armonica (musical instrument), 74–75, 96

The Art of Swimming (unknown), 18–19

asbestos, 29

astronomy, 37, 76

aurora borealis, 94

Bailly, Jean-Sylvain, 97

balloons, 94–96

Bartram, John, 37

bathtubs, 80, *81*

batteries, 94, 108

beer, 33

Beethoven, Ludwig van, 75

bifocal eyeglasses, 73–74, *74*

birth of Franklin, 11, 17

Boston, Massachusetts, 17

Boston Harbor, 21

Boston Tea Party, 88

botany, 37

Boulton, Matthew, 87, 108

Boyle, Robert, 15, 36, 37

Bunyan, John, 18

candle-making, 18, 21

catheter invention, 71

charge, electrical, 54

charm of Franklin, 92

chemistry, 15, 23, 93–94

chess, 93

childbirth, 11

Christ's Church, Philadelphia, 63

Church of England, 20

Civil War, 82

climate change, 77, 110

cloud discharge, 60. *See also* lightning

coiffure à la Franklin, 92

Colonies
  and the American Revolution, 88–89,
    99
  diseases and epidemics in, 11–12, 13,
    15, 24, 38, 90, 104
  politics of, 85–89
  state of science in, 11–12
color theory, 74
Committee of Five, 88
common-law marriage, 34
conduction of electricity, 59–69
conservation of charge, 54
Constitutional Convention, 101–2
controlled experimentation, 97–98
Copley Medal, 68
The Courant, 25

"The Dangling Boy" (performance), 51
Darwin, Erasmus, 87
Davy, Humphrey, 108
death of Franklin, 103–5
Declaration of Independence, 88
deism, 23
democratic theory, 101–2
demographics, 77
Descartes, René, 67
diplomatic missions
  to France, 90–98
  to Great Britain, 86–89
diseases and epidemics, 11–12, 13, 15, 24,
    38–39, 90, 104
Dissertations on the English Language
  (Webster), 36
Dogood, Silence (pseudonym), 23, 25
Du Fay, Charles François de Cisternay, 52
Dutch ovens, 44

ecology, 73
education
  formal education of Franklin, 20–21

honorary degrees of Franklin, 78
self-education of Franklin, 14, 15,
    18–19, 23–24, 32, 36, 107
standards in the Colonies, 11
of women, 35, 82–83
electricity
  charge concept, 54
  conduction of, 59–69
  early theories of, 50–52
  electromagnetism theory, 109
  electrons, 110
  "electrophore" machine, 94
  experiments in Great Britain, 87
  fame of Franklin, 10
  fluid theory of, 14, 51–52
  Franklin's research on, 49–58, 59–69
  friction machines, 98
  and grounding, 55–56, 66–69
  kite experiment, 63
  legacy of Franklin, 13–14, 105
  Leyden jars, 15, 53–57, 60, 64, 94,
    106, 108
  as light source, 109
  shock therapy, 71–72
Elizabeth I of England, 50
Enlightenment, 12, 23
Every Man His Own Doctor (Tennant), 36
evolution, 110
exercise, 73
experimentation
  and debunking frauds, 97–98
  and electricity research, 52–54, 57–58,
    59–69, 63, 87, 106, 107
  and heating systems, 42–43, 46
  and Newton's *Opticks*, 16
  regard for Franklin's work, 37–38,
    56–57, 58, 95
  and scope of Franklin's interests,
    74–78
Experiments and Observations of

Electricity (Franklin), 57–58, 107
extinction, 77
eyeglasses, 73–74, 74

fame of Franklin, 91–92
Faraday, Michael, 109
fireplaces, 43–44
fires, 12
flippers for swimming, 19
fluid theory of electricity, 14, 51–52
flying machines, 94–96
food safety, 72, 95
fossils, 76–77
Founding Fathers, 35, 100, 102
founding of the U.S., 10, 11, 16
France
    and electricity research, 51–52, 65,
        67–68
    Franco-American alliance, 93, 98
    Franklin's diplomatic mission to, 90–98
    regard for Franklin in, 103–4
Franklin, Abiah, 17, 18
Franklin, Benjamin
    birth of, 11, 17
    charm of, 92
    death of, 103–5
    formal education of, 20–21
    marriage of, 34
    and printing/publishing, 22–23
    self-education and improvement of, 14,
        15, 18–19, 23–24, 32, 36, 107
    work ethic of, 28, 30
    See also specific topics throughout index
Franklin, Deborah
    death, 88
    and Franklin's overseas travels, 85–86
    and lightning rods, 68
    marriage, 34–35
    relationship with Franklin, 34–35, 83,
        86

and slavery, 82
Franklin, Ebenezer, 18
Franklin, Francis ("Franky"), 35
Franklin, James, 15, 22, 25, 28
Franklin, John, 70–71
Franklin, Josiah, 14, 17–18, 20–21
Franklin, Josiah, Jr., 21
Franklin, Sally, 47, 83, 84
Franklin, William
    and Franklin's death, 103
    and Franklin's marriage, 34–35
    and the kite experiment, 63–69, 106
    loyalism of, 88
Franklin stove, 44–47
franklinistes, 91–92
friction machines, 98
frugality of Franklin, 20, 23
funeral of Franklin, 104

gender discrimination, 82–83
George (slave), 82
George II of England, 54
germ theory, 72
Germans, 80
Gilbert, William, 50
gout, 102
grammar-school education, 20–21
Gray, Stephen, 50
Great Britain, 85–89
Greek philosophy, 50
ground, electrical, 55–56, 66–69
Guillotine, Ignace, 97
Gulf Stream, 75–76, 100, 110

Halley, Edmond, 37
Harvard College, 20–21
Harvey, William, 13, 15, 42
health care, 70–71, 80. *See also* medicine
health problems of Franklin, 32, 38–39,
    102

heating systems, 41–47

Henry, Patrick, 86–87

The History and Present State of Electricity (Priestley), 65

home of Franklin (Philadelphia), 83

home-heating designs, 42

honorary degrees, 78

hospitals, 11, 72–73

humor of Franklin, 13, 79–80

hydrogen balloons, 95–96

immunization, 15, 24–25, 34, 38–39, 90, 104

indentured servitude, 22

independence movement
and the American Revolution, 88–89, 90–91, 98, 99
and Franklin's mission to Great Britain, 85–89
Franklin's support for, 11, 49
and the printing business, 22–23

Industrial Age, 108

infant mortality, 17–18

inoculations, 15, 24–25, 34, 38–39, 90, 104

insect behavior, 76–77

insulation, electrical, 56, 61–63, 62

inventions, 19

Islam, 78

Jefferson, Thomas, 89, 100, 102–3

Jemima (slave), 82

the Junto, 33, 35–36, 38, 46

Kinnersley, Ebenezer, 53

kite experiment, 63, 63–69, 106

Lavoisier, Antoine, 93–94, 97

lawmaking, 38

lead poisoning, 71

legacy of Franklin, 105–11

lending libraries, 35–36

Leonardo da Vinci, 13

Leyden jars
creator of, 15
described, 53
and Franklin's electricity research, 53–57, 60, 64, 106
improvements on, 94, 108

libraries, 11, 35–36, 83–84

lighting systems, 77, 91, 109

lightning
and Franklin's publishing, 34
Franklin's research on, 59–69
lightning rods, 14, 66–69, 87, 100, 104, 108
photographed, 110

Logan, James, 37

London, England, 28–29, 73

Louis XV, 65

Louis XVI, 92

loyalism, 88

lunar eclipses, 76

Lunar Society of Birmingham, 87, 108

Marum, Martinus van, 98

Massachusetts, 20

mathematics, 12, 21, 23, 36

Mather, Cotton, 14, 20, 24, 32

Maxwell, James Clerk, 109

measles, 14

medicine
and early colonial era, 11
electric shock therapy, 71–72
and Franklin's health problems, 32, 38–39, 102
and Franklin's publishing, 36
and Franklin's self-education, 15
and germ theory, 72
and inoculations, 15, 24–25, 34, 38–39, 90, 104
and lead poisoning, 71

medical school founded, 78
and scientific advance, 12–13
memorial service for Franklin, 103–4
mental illness, 72–73
Mesmer, Franz, 96
mesmerism, 96–98
meteorology, 76
Montgolfier brothers, 94–95
Morse, Samuel, 109
motion pictures, 109
Mozart, Wolfgang Amadeus, 75
music, 74–75, 84

natural disasters, 12
natural philosophy
and electricity research, 57
and Franklin's curiosity, 30–31, 47
and Franklin's legacy, 11
and Franklin's sea travels, 99–100
naval architecture, 99–100
navigation, 75–76
networking skills of Franklin, 37
The New-England Courant, 22–23
New York City, 26, 27
newspaper publishing, 22–23, 29, 33, 46
Newton, Isaac
and fluid theory of electricity, 51–52
Franklin compared to, 69
and Franklin's humor, 79
Franklin's reverence for, 14–15, 16,
24, 44, 48
and Opticks, 16, 73–74
and Poor Richard's Almanack, 37
and the Scientific Revolution, 10,
12–13
Nollet, Jean-Antoine, 51, 67–68
Northern Lights, 94

oceanic current, 75–76
one-hundred-dollar bill, 107

Onesimus, 24
opium, 102–3
Opticks (Newton), 16, 73–74
Othello (slave), 82

paddles (for swimming), 19
paleontology, 77
parlor tricks, 51
particle physics, 110
Pasteur, Louis, 72
patents, 67
Pennsylvania Abolition Society, 82
Pennsylvania Assembly, 38, 58, 85
"Pennsylvania fireplace," 46
The Pennsylvania Gazette, 33–34
Pennsylvania Hospital, 72–73
perspiration, 80
Peter (slave), 82
Philadelphia, Pennsylvania
and the American Philosophical
Society, 37–38
Common Council, 49
Franklin's arrival in, 27–28
and Franklin's legacy, 107
Franklin's return to, 32, 99–100
and the independence movement, 49
and the printing business, 30
streetlamps, 77
phonograph, 109
physics
and Franklin's legacy, 10, 110
and Franklin's self-education, 23
and Franklin's stove design, 44–46
and the Scientific Revolution, 12–13
physiology, 42
Pierce, Franklin, 107
The Pilgrim's Progress (Bunyan), 18
placebo effect, 97
"A Plan for Future Conduct" (Franklin),
30

Pliny the Elder, 50
pluralism, 78
politics
    accomplishments of Franklin, 16
    and Franklin's diplomatic missions,
        85–89, 90–98
    and Franklin's printing business, 38
    and public service of Franklin, 48
    See also independence movement
pollution, 73
Poor Richard's Almanack (Franklin),
    36–37, 67, 104
population growth, 17, 24, 77
portable bathtubs, 80, *81*
preventive medicine, 73
Priestley, Joseph, 65, 68–69, 87
Principia Mathematica (Newton), 16, 37
Pringle, John, 87
printing business
    and Franklin's apprenticeship, 22–25
    Franklin's first shop, 33–34
    and Franklin's political career, 38
    Franklin's retirement from, 47, 48
    and Franklin's trade, 11
    and Franklin's writing skills, 15
    and Franklin's writings, 58
    and the independence movement,
        22–23
    and lead poisoning, 71
    and London, 30
    and medical books, 36
    and Philadelphia, 28–29, 32–33
Protestantism, 20
pseudonyms of Franklin, 23
public health and safety, 11–12, 14,
    17–18, 72. *See also* lightning; medicine
public life of Franklin, 48. *See also* politics
public speaking, 48–49
publishing business, 11, 15, 46, 47
Puritans, 14, 20, 23
Pythagoras, 104

racism, 80
rationalism, 13, 30, 89
Read, Deborah, 34–35
reading, 18
refrigeration, 72
religion
    and deism, 23
    and Franklin's education, 20–21
    and rationalism, 89
    and reaction to lightning rods, 67–68
religious freedom, 20
religious pluralism, 78
Revolutionary War, 88–89, 90–98, 99
Roman Catholic Church, 20
Roosevelt, Franklin, 107
Royal Society
    and the Copley Medal, 68
    and Cotton Mather, 20
    and Franklin's electricity research, 57
    Franklin's letters to, 14, 38
    and Franklin's time in London, 28–29,
        87
    and French balloon craze, 95

Salem witchcraft trials, 12, 14
sayings of Franklin, 37
science
    and Cotton Mather, 14
    and curiosity of Franklin, 70–78
    and deism, 23
    and Franklin's legacy, 108
    and Franklin's mission to France,
        92–98
    and Franklin's stove design, 41–47
    and frauds, 96–98
    and newspaper publishing, 33–34
    and Newton's *Opticks*, 16
    rate of scientific advance, 10–11,
        33–34, 96, 108
    and rationalism, 12–13
    regard for Franklin's work, 37–38,

56–57, 58, 95
and the Royal Society, 20
scientific journals, 15, 29, 30, 46
scientific method, 16, 41
Scientific Revolution, 12
"scientist" term, 105
See also experimentation; medicine
scurvy, 72
shock therapy, 71–72
skepticism, 97–98
slavery, 35, 82
smallpox, 11–12, 15, 24, 38, 90, 104
soap making, 18
social skills of Franklin, 37
The Spectator, 23–24
speeches of Franklin, 48–49
Spencer, Archibald, 49
St. Mark's Basilica, 67
Stamp Act, 86–87
static electricity, 50–51, 53, 98
steam engines, 108
Stevenson, Margaret, 83
Stevenson, Polly, 83
stoves, 13, 41–47
streetlamps, 77
Sundry Maritime Observations
(Franklin), 100
superstition
and left-handedness, 20
and lightning, 59–60
and reaction to lightning rods, 67–68
and the Salem witchcraft trials, 12, 14
swimming, 18–19, *19*, 29–30

Tampa Bay, Florida, 110
taxation, 86–87
telegraph, 109
Thales of Miletus, 50
theories, scientific, 10, 16
Thomson, J. J., 110
trades, 21–22

University of Pennsylvania, 78
urinary catheter invention, 71
U.S. Congress, 82, 98, 101–2
U.S. Constitution, 101–2
U.S. House of Representatives, 101–2
U.S. Senate, 101–2

vaccination (inoculation), 15, 24–25, 34,
38–39, 90, 104
Van Musschenbroek, Pieter, 15, 54,
56–57
"Venus Electrificata," 51
virtues of Franklin, 30
vision, 73–74
vitamin C deficiency, 72
Volta, Alessandro, 94, 108

Warden of the Mint, 48
Washington, George, 90, 100
Watt, James, 87, 108
weather, 76. *See also* lightning
Webster, Noah, 36
Wedgwood, Josiah, 87
wine, 92
witchcraft, 12, 14
women, 82–83
woodburning stoves, 43–47
work ethic of Franklin, 28, 30
writings of Franklin
*Account of the New Invented
Pennsylvanian Fire-Places*, 46
and diplomatic mission to France, 94
*Experiments and Observations of
Electricity*, 57–58, 107
Poor Richard's Almanack, 36–37, 67,
104
and self-education, 23–24
"Silence Dogood" letters, 23, 25
Sundry Maritime Observations, 100